The
Missouri Compromise

by Michael Burgan

Content Adviser: Lewis Gould, Professor Emeritus,
Department of History,
University of Texas at Austin

Reading Adviser: Susan Kesselring, M.A.,
Literacy Educator,
Rosemount–Apple Valley–Eagan (Minnesota) School District

COMPASS POINT BOOKS
MINNEAPOLIS, MINNESOTA

Compass Point Books
3109 West 50th Street, #115
Minneapolis, MN 55410

Visit Compass Point Books on the Internet at *www.compasspointbooks.com*
or e-mail your request to *custserv@compasspointbooks.com*

On the cover: A group of slaves held in chains passes the unfinished Capitol building in
Washington, D.C., circa 1820.

Photographs ©: The Granger Collection, New York, cover, 15, 19, 30, 31; Prints Old and Rare,
back cover (far left); Library of Congress, back cover, 8, 13, 16, 24, 26, 36; U.S. Senate Art
Collection, *Thomas Jefferson* by Thomas Sully, 4; North Wind Picture Archives, 5, 7, 10, 12, 17,
21, 33, 38; MPI/Getty Images, 9, 27; Hulton Archive/Getty Images, 14; Stock Montage/Getty
Images, 20; Corbis, 23; Bettmann/Corbis, 35; Michael Masian Historic Photographs/Corbis, 37;
Stock Montage, Inc., 40, 41.

Editor: Nick Healy
Page Production: Bobbie Nuytten
Photo Researcher: Marcie C. Spence
Cartographer: XNR Productions, Inc.
Library Consultant: Kathleen Baxter

Creative Director: Keith Griffin
Editorial Director: Carol Jones
Managing Editor: Catherine Neitge

Library of Congress Cataloging-in-Publication Data
Burgan, Michael.
  The Missouri compromise / by Michael Burgan.
      p. cm.—(We the people)
  Includes bibliographical references and index.
  ISBN 0-7565-1634-X (hard cover)
  ISBN 0-7565-1769-9 (paperback)
  1. Missouri compromise—Juvenile literature. 2. Slavery—United States—History—Juvenile litera-
ture. 3. United States—Politics and government—1815-1861—Juvenile literature. I. Title. II. We the
people (Series) (Compass Point Books)
  E373.B89 2006
  973.7'113—dc22   2005025086

TABLE OF CONTENTS

TENSE TIMES IN WASHINGTON, D.C.

It was 1820, and former President Thomas Jefferson had grown worried. He saw how slavery was dividing his country. From afar, he watched Congress battle over the future of Missouri. He was troubled by the fight in Washington, D.C., over whether to allow slavery in this new state on the Western frontier. He called the matter "a firebell in the night [that] awakened and filled me with terror."

The Civil War was more than 40 years away. But already one of the nation's founders

Portrait of Thomas Jefferson by Thomas Sully

4

feared slavery would rip apart the United States.

Jefferson and others had good reason to worry. In 1819 and 1820, harsh language and hot tempers filled the halls of the U.S. Capitol. Arguments arose among senators and representatives in Congress. Their branch of the government made the country's laws, and they were considering a plan to grant statehood to the Missouri Territory.

Missouri merchants shipped goods along the Mississippi River on flatboats.

The Missouri Territory was part of the Western land the United States had purchased from France in 1803. Missouri had been carved out of the larger Louisiana Territory. Now the people of Missouri wanted to form a state and enter the Union.

Many Northerners opposed the spread of slavery into new states joining the Union. Slavery forced black people to live under the control of their white masters. Slaves were forced to work without pay. They were barred from the simple freedom to come and go as they pleased. Often they were forbidden from learning to read and write. They were punished harshly for breaking the rules. Their lives were full of suffering.

As far back as 1783, Northern states had begun to outlaw slavery and to call for its gradual end. Lawmakers from the North did not want to see slavery grow, especially to new states such as Missouri.

Most Southern lawmakers thought Missouri should be allowed to permit slavery. They argued that residents of

Debate over Missouri led to tense disputes in the U.S. Congress.

Missouri already owned slaves. Also, slaveholders from Southern states hoped to settle in Missouri someday, bringing their slaves with them. The South's economy was tied to raising crops such as cotton, rice, sugar, and tobacco. Southern plantation owners relied on slaves to plant, tend, and harvest these crops.

7

William Plumer Jr.

The debate over Missouri concerned leaders in the capital, including William Plumer Jr. of New Hampshire. Plumer was a member of the U.S. House of Representatives. In a letter to his father, Plumer wrote that "rage and fury ... have prevailed here on this subject," which he called the "Missouri Question." And the current president, James Monroe, shared the worries of his friend Jefferson. In a letter to Jefferson, Monroe wrote that he had "never known a question so menacing," or dangerous, to the nation.

FROM TERRITORY TO STATE

With the Louisiana Purchase, the United States doubled in size. Most residents of the Louisiana Territory lived in and around the city of New Orleans. Under French rule, slavery was legal there, and many slaves worked on sugar plantations outside the city.

In 1803, Americans James Monroe, a future president, and Robert Livingston reached terms for the Louisiana Purchase with the French foreign minister.

9

Thomas Jefferson, who backed the Louisiana Purchase, was U.S. president at the time. He rejected the suggestion of a Connecticut lawmaker that slavery be made illegal in the Louisiana Territory. Jefferson had already agreed to allow slavery in Louisiana. He saw it as a right allowed by the U.S. Constitution. He also realized that

An 1803 map of the United States showing the new Louisiana Territory

slave owners from Southern states might one day want to move into the new territory.

During the next decade, many slaveholders were among the settlers in Missouri. They came from elsewhere in the Louisiana Territory and from Southern states. In addition, some slaves had arrived in Missouri earlier with French Canadian settlers. Most of the newcomers made their homes in St. Louis or other settlements along the Mississippi River.

By 1818, Missouri had enough residents to apply for statehood. That April, Congress began debating a bill that would make Missouri a state. Given the number of slave owners who lived there, most people assumed Missouri would permit slavery once it became a state. However, some Northern lawmakers did not want slavery to be legalized in Missouri.

As members of Congress considered the Missouri bill, Representative Arthur Livermore of New Hampshire made a proposal. He wanted to change the U.S. Constitution.

Plantation owners inspect slaves to be sold at auction in New Orleans.

His amendment called for a ban on slavery in any new state joining the Union. Congress rejected Livermore's idea. Still, Missouri statehood and the future of slavery had been linked for good. There would be no separating the two issues.

12

INTENSE DEBATE BEGINS

Congress did not act on the 1818 bill calling for Missouri statehood. However, lawmakers began debating a second statehood bill in February 1819. Almost immediately, Representative James Tallmadge Jr. of New York tried to change the bill. Like many Northerners at the time, Tallmadge was troubled by slavery. He called it an example of "suffering human nature."

Missouri settlers lived in log cabins on the frontier.

Tallmadge said that Missouri should become a state only if no more slaves were brought there. He also said the children of the current slaves should be freed when they became adults. These two notions formed the basis of his proposed amendment to the statehood bill. The Tallmadge amendment led "to an interesting and pretty wide debate," one lawmaker said.

Tallmadge later wrote that he did not expect Congress to accept his proposal. He did hope, however, to "have produced moral effects which will eventually [save] our beloved country from disgrace and danger." To Tallmadge and other Northerners, slavery caused that disgrace and danger.

14

James Tallmadge Jr.

In Congress, other Northern lawmakers supported Tallmadge. Some, like him, saw slavery as a moral issue. They believed it was wrong for one human to claim others as property and deny them their freedom.

Other Tallmadge supporters said slavery and its future in the West was only a legal issue. The Constitution said Congress had a duty to make sure new states had republican governments. In this form of government, voters elect people to represent them. If Missouri allowed slavery, then some of its citizens— the slaves—would not be

SPEECH

OF

THE HONORABLE

JAMES TALLMADGE, Jr.

OF

Duchess County, New-York,

IN THE

House of Representatives of the United States,

ON

SLAVERY.

TO WHICH IS ADDED, THE PROCEEDINGS OF THE

MANUMISSION SOCIETY

OF THE CITY OF NEW-YORK,

AND THE

CORRESPONDENCE OF THEIR COMMITTEE

WITH

Messrs. Tallmadge and Taylor.

NEW-YORK:

PRINTED BY E. CONRAD,

Frankfort-street.

1819.

The cover of a printed copy of Tallmadge's speech in Congress calling for a gradual end to slavery in Missouri

15

Philip Barbour

allowed to vote. The government would not be truly republican, according to slavery's opponents.

At the same time, many lawmakers said they did not want to end slavery where it already existed. But from then on, they said, the country should not allow slavery in new states.

Southerners attacked Tallmadge's amendment. Representative Philip Barbour of Virginia said Missouri and other new states had to be allowed to decide for themselves what to do about slavery. Henry Clay of Kentucky was also against the amendment. He was the Speaker of the House, the most powerful person in the House of Representatives, and like many Southern members of Congress, he owned slaves. Yet he

16

also thought slavery was wrong and should end—slowly. However, Clay thought the people of Missouri who already owned slaves had a right to keep them.

On both sides, lawmakers saw sectionalism at work. With sectionalism, people pursued goals that would help their section of the country and, possibly, hurt another. The North and South saw each other as separate sections with different needs and interests.

Slavery was a major source of disagreement between the two sections. However, it was just one of several issues that divided them. In general, Northerners supported laws that helped merchants and industry. Their economy

The rise of industry led to the growth of Northern cities.

17

relied on making goods and trading with other nations. Southerners wanted to help farmers sell cotton and other crops. They believed slavery was vital to their economy.

Southerners believed attacks on slavery were Northern sectionalism at work. Hugh Nelson of Virginia wrote that the North wanted "to exclude all the Southern people from migrating to [Missouri]." If Congress passed the amendment, slave owners could not move there with their slaves.

Northern leaders saw a political danger to their region if slavery spread. As the country had grown, Southern and Western states gained power and Northern states lost some influence. Northerners feared the South gained power every time a slave state joined the Union.

Like today, the number of representatives in the U.S. House was based on a state's population. In 1819, the population of Southern states included slaves. (However, each slave counted as only three-fifths of a person.) As the slave population grew in Southern states, the overall popu-

The chamber of the United States House of Representatives in the 1820s

lation in the region grew faster than the population in the North. And so did the number of Southern representatives. Northerners thought that new slave states would elect pro-slavery lawmakers to Congress. In turn, they would pass laws that helped Southern states and, possibly, hurt Northern states. Consequently, the North would have less chance of limiting or ending slavery. All this strengthened the North's support for the Tallmadge amendment.

The House of Representatives voted separately on the two parts of Tallmadge's proposal. By a vote of 87-76, the representatives said that no new slaves could be

Rufus King

brought into Missouri. Members voted 82-78 to gradually free the children of existing slaves. In both votes, almost all Northern lawmakers supported Tallmadge. Almost all the Southerners opposed him.

The bill for Missouri statehood now went to the U.S. Senate. Rufus King of New York led the Northerners. He repeated many of the arguments that had been made in the House. The Senate, however, voted to reject the Tallmadge amendment, so the Missouri bill went back to the House. Lawmakers in that chamber refused to reconsider the bill with the antislavery language in the amendment removed. Congress soon ended its session. The Missouri bill was dead—for a time.

COMING TO A COMPROMISE

During the summer and fall of 1819, the Missouri issue sparked strong antislavery feelings in the North. More and more citizens demanded Congress forbid slavery in Missouri. They argued that the men who created the U.S. Constitution in 1787 never wanted slavery to expand. They expected it to remain legal only where it existed at that

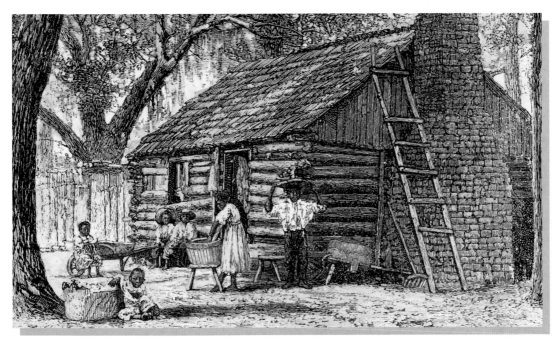

Settlers from the South brought slaves to the Missouri Territory.

21

time. One New York newspaper wrote, "This question involves not only the future character of our nation, but the future ... influence of the free states. If now lost—it is lost forever."

A new issue soon became part of the Missouri Question. For more than 100 years, Maine had been part of Massachusetts. But people in Maine were frustrated by the decisions made in the faraway state capital of Boston. During the summer of 1819, Massachusetts lawmakers decided to let Maine become a separate state. But they set a deadline for action of March 4, 1820. Now Congress had to consider bills for letting both Maine and Missouri enter the Union.

Congress met again in December 1819. One of its first acts was to form a committee to study the Missouri Question. Leaders hoped to find a compromise that both the North and South would accept. The committee, however, failed to reach an agreement.

Soon after, the House and Senate each considered

An escaped slave leaps from a building rather than allowing herself to be captured and returned to her owners.

bills for allowing Maine into the Union. Slavery was illegal in Maine, and residents planned to enter the Union as a free state. As 1820 began, the United States had 11 slave states and 11 free states. Southerners wanted to keep that even balance of slave and free states. Henry Clay warned that Maine's request to enter the Union could be rejected by Southerners if Northerners were to "refuse to admit Missouri also free of condition."

In January 1820, the House passed a bill granting Maine statehood. The Senate then attached Missouri's statehood to the bill. Under the Senate plan, Missouri would come in without a limit on slavery. The Senate also added a new idea to the debate.

Speaker of the House Henry Clay

Senators proposed drawing an imaginary boundary along the southern border of Missouri. This boundary was on the 36 degrees 30 minutes line of latitude. Slavery would be illegal in any part of the Louisiana Purchase above that line—except in Missouri. Below that line, citizens could own slaves, if they chose. Southern senators said this would keep slavery out of future Western territories and states.

The key points of the Senate's plan, which included statehood for Maine and Missouri, would become known as the Missouri Compromise. Senators hoped that their new limit on slavery in the West would win the support of Northerners in the House.

The Northern representatives, however, did not like the idea. They rejected linking the statehood of Maine and Missouri. They also did not support the 36 degrees 30 minutes boundary. And many lawmakers still wanted to limit slavery in Missouri. Once again, neither the House nor the Senate would give in.

For months, President James Monroe had closely watched the ongoing debate. Monroe was a Southerner and a slave owner. Like Henry Clay, he disliked slavery, but he did not think it could be ended right away. He also believed that Congress should "have no right to admit in

25

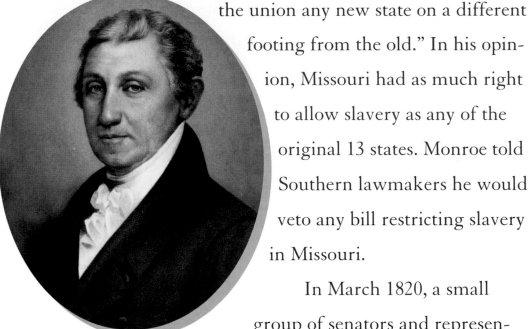

President James Monroe

the union any new state on a different footing from the old." In his opinion, Missouri had as much right to allow slavery as any of the original 13 states. Monroe told Southern lawmakers he would veto any bill restricting slavery in Missouri.

In March 1820, a small group of senators and representatives held a conference. Clay wanted all of Congress to accept the Missouri Compromise. For the conference, he chose members of the House who he thought would also support a compromise. Clay and other lawmakers feared trouble if Congress did not settle the issue soon.

Some people from both the North and South were talking about disunion—the splitting of the United States into two or more separate countries. A few lawmakers even

Henry Clay addresses the members of the U.S. Senate.

suggested the issue could lead to violence. Senator Freeman
Walker of Georgia imagined what might happen one day:
"The father [would be] armed against the son, and the son
against the father" as the country battled over slavery.

In their conference, the Senate and House members
suggested three key points. One, Congress should decide
separately if Maine and Missouri should be states. Two, no
limits should be placed on slavery in Missouri. And three,
the 36 degrees 30 minutes line should limit slavery in
the future.

By separating the main issues, Congress could debate and vote on each point separately. Clay and the others knew this meant there was a greater chance that all three would pass. And this would prevent Northern lawmakers who opposed slavery in Missouri from uniting with Southerners who opposed limits on slavery. Together, they

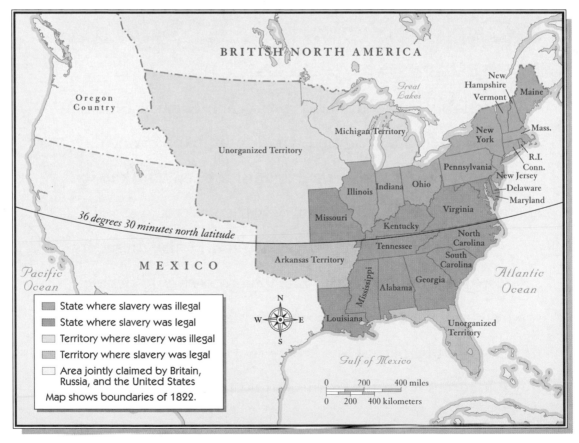

Slavery was limited under the Missouri Compromise.

would have defeated a single bill that linked all of the issues.

After nearly two years of debate, Congress passed the Missouri Compromise. The closest vote on the separate bills came in the House in March 1820. Its members voted 90-87 to admit Missouri as a slave state. Some Northerners voted for this, perhaps to make sure Southerners would accept the boundary.

The voting by Northerners was complicated by party loyalties. Some Northerners were Democrats, who believed in a weaker central government that allowed states more power. The Democrats wanted states like Missouri to decide for themselves if they would allow slavery, so they opposed any limits on slavery in Missouri. Most Northerners, however, belonged to the other major party, the Federalists, who believed the national government had every right to limit slavery in Missouri. The Northern Democrats did not want to support the Federalists on a key issue like this.

29

William Plumer Jr. was one Northern Democrat who did not change his mind. He voted against allowing Missouri to enter as a slave state. He said others who changed their minds to vote for slavery were "weak-minded." However, Plumer was pleased slavery had been limited in other Western lands. The compromise was worth "more than all the trouble it has cost us, the time we have spent, and the unkind feelings which have been excited."

An 1820s political cartoon on Western settlement shows Democrats atop a westward facing alligator while their political opponents ride a tortoise looking east.

A Second Compromise

After all that, the fight over Missouri was not over. The bill granting statehood to Missouri did not allow it to immediately enter the Union. First, people there had to draft a state constitution. Then Congress had to approve this document to officially make Missouri a state. By law, Missouri's state constitution could not conflict with the U.S. Constitution.

The cabin that was home to Missouri's first governor, Alexander McNair, in 1820

During the summer of 1820, Missouri worked on its constitution. One part of it angered Northerners who opposed slavery. Missouri's proposed constitution would have prevented free African-Americans from settling in the state. In some states, free blacks were considered citizens, and under the U.S. Constitution, all citizens, including free blacks, had a right to move from state to state.

In fact, Missouri was proposing a constitution that violated the U.S. Constitution. Antislavery leaders thought they now had a reason to keep Missouri out of the Union.

Still, Missouri had strong support in the U.S. Senate. Almost every senator from the South supported Missouri's constitution. Several Northern senators who had been born in the South also approved the document.

But in December 1820, the House of Representatives voted against accepting Missouri's constitution. Some lawmakers said they would not change their minds until Missourians agreed to let free blacks settle there like other citizens.

The vote angered the people of Missouri and many Southerners. Some lawmakers talked of repealing the Missouri Compromise. Once again, people warned of disunion or violence. And once again, Henry Clay stepped forward to try to find a compromise. Clay was no longer

Settlers at Choteau's Pond, now part of St. Louis, Missouri

Speaker of the House, but lawmakers still respected him. He held a series of conferences to try to win approval for the constitution.

The presidential election of 1820 added to the problems. James Monroe had clearly won enough electoral votes to serve again as president. Electoral votes are cast by special electors. Each state has the same number of electors as it does members of Congress. Since Missouri claimed it was already a state, it sent three electors to Washington, D.C.

Some Northerners said those votes could not be counted because Missouri was not yet legally a state. A heated debate broke out in Congress when a Southern senator tried to record Missouri's three votes in the final result. Clay suggested that two counts be taken: one with Missouri's votes and one without. In either case, Monroe was still president.

Some Southern lawmakers, however, continued to howl. They wanted Congress to declare once and for all that Missouri was a state. William Plumer Jr. wrote that

James Monroe is sworn in as president of the United States.

John Floyd of Virginia protested "in the most violent manner, with menacing gestures, and in a tone of defiance and rage, exceeding anything I ever saw."

By now, lawmakers were tired of the whole Missouri issue. For months, they had hardly talked about anything else. They had spent long hours in debate, without even breaking for meals. Clay tried one last time to win the House's approval for the Missouri constitution. He called

35

John B. Floyd

for a committee of House and Senate members to discuss what to do.

Clay suggested they approve an idea discussed earlier in the House. Missouri would be allowed into the Union with the proposed constitution. But the state's lawmakers would have to accept one limit on their actions. They would be forbidden from passing laws that denied citizens of other states the rights protected by the U.S. Constitution. In effect, Missouri could not deny the rights of free blacks, despite what the state's constitution said.

Clay's strategy worked. On February 26, the House voted 87-81 to let Missouri enter the Union. Eighteen

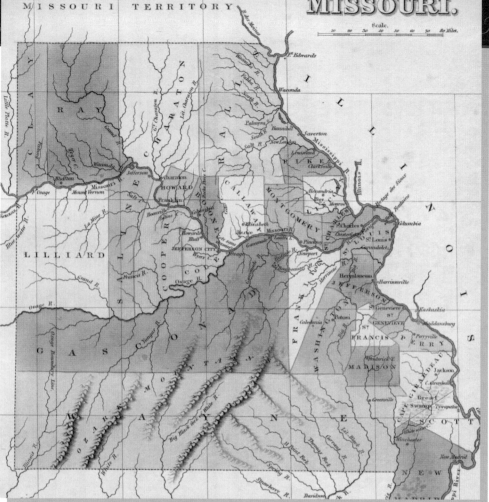

An 1826 map of the state of Missouri

Northern representatives voted for the bill. Within a few
days, the Senate also approved it. In June, Missouri's lawmakers agreed to accept the limit Congress had placed on
them. Finally, Missouri officially entered the Union on
August 10, 1821, as the 24th state.

AFTER THE COMPROMISE

The Missouri Question had deeply divided Congress. Two compromises finally helped to solve conflicts relating to that one state. However, slavery continued to pit the North against the South.

In the 1830s, a pro-slavery riot led to the burning of an antislavery publisher's shop.

During the 1830s, abolitionists, who were people opposed to slavery, demanded an immediate end to slavery everywhere in the United States. Over the next two decades, Northerners tried again to limit the spread of slavery in new territories and states. Southerners, meanwhile, argued that citizens had a right to decide for themselves if they wanted slavery.

For years, some Southerners considered the Missouri Compromise an insult to them. They thought they had been unfairly forced to accept a limit on their legal rights. In 1854, they managed to repeal part of the Missouri Compromise of 1820. Congress passed the Kansas-Nebraska Act, which allowed slavery above the 36 degrees 30 minutes line in lands that had been part of the Louisiana Purchase. Tension between the North and South grew, and the talk of disunion that had filled Congress in 1820 returned.

The election of President Abraham Lincoln in 1860 angered many people in the South who feared slavery

A Southerner waves a flag supporting South Carolina's move to leave the Union.

would be restricted. This time, Congress could not reach any compromise on the issue. Southern states, led by South Carolina, seceded—or withdrew—from the Union. The South declared itself a separate nation and began a bloody war between North and South.

Lincoln would not let the Union crumble. He led

the nation through the Civil War and proclaimed all slaves free. The war stretched over four bloody years. With the North's victory and the adoption of the 13th Amendment in 1865, slavery finally ended forever in the United States.

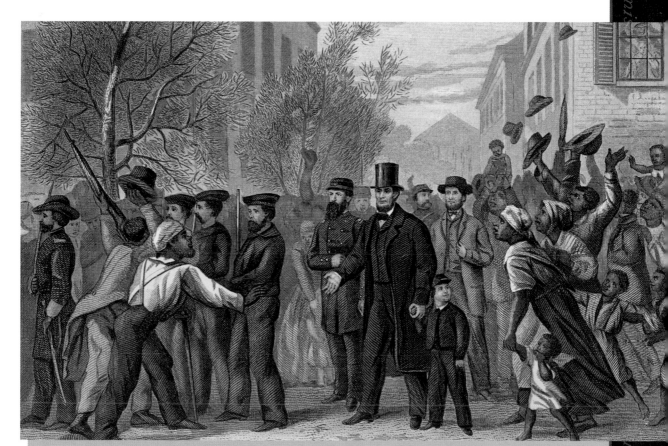

A freed slave greets President Lincoln during the last days of the Civil War.

GLOSSARY

abolitionists—people who supported the banning of slavery

amendment—a formal change made to a law or legal document, such as a constitution

constitution—a document stating the basic rules of a government

latitude—distance measured north or south of the equator; each degree of latitude equals about 69 miles (110 kilometers)

plantation—large farm in the South, usually worked by slaves

repeal—to officially cancel something, such as a law

sectionalism—making political decisions based on what is good for one region over another

veto—refuse to approve, which prevents a measure from becoming law

DID YOU KNOW?

- Thanks to his efforts on the Missouri Question, Henry Clay was nicknamed "The Great Compromiser." Clay ran for U.S. president several times but never won.

- In 1820, Missouri had a population of about 66,000, which included about 11,000 slaves.

- William Plumer Jr.'s letters about the Missouri Compromise were written to his father, who had also served in Congress.

- The Kansas-Nebraska Act of 1854 repealed the 36 degrees 30 minutes boundary limiting slavery. That law created the territory of Kansas out of Nebraska and allowed settlers in both territories to decide for themselves if they wanted slavery.

- In 1857, the U.S. Supreme Court ruled in the Dred Scott case that laws such as the Missouri Compromise violated the Constitution. The Supreme Court said Congress had no power to limit slavery in Western territories. The ruling outraged people in the North and moved the nation closer to the Civil War.

IMPORTANT DATES

Timeline

1803 The United States buys the Louisiana Territory from France.

1818 Missouri asks Congress to be admitted as a state.

1819 In February, Representative James Tallmadge Jr. calls for limits on slavery in Missouri; in March, the Senate and House of Representatives split on the proposal.

1820 Congress agrees to the Missouri Compromise, allowing slavery in Missouri but preventing the spread of slavery above the 36 degrees 30 minutes line; in December, Missouri submits a constitution to Congress, which the House of Representatives rejects.

1821 Congress grants Missouri statehood with the condition that none of its laws deny citizens of other states their rights under the U.S. Constitution.

1854 Congress passes the Kansas-Nebraska Act, repealing the part of the Missouri Compromise that limited slavery north of the 36 degrees 30 minutes line.

IMPORTANT PEOPLE

PHILIP BARBOUR (1783–1841)

U.S. representative from Virginia who opposed placing any limits on slavery in Missouri and was later elected Speaker of the House

HENRY CLAY (1777–1852)

Kentucky lawmaker and Speaker of the House of Representatives during the first debate over Missouri; a major supporter of the Missouri Compromise

RUFUS KING (1755–1827)

U.S. senator from New York who led Northern lawmakers opposed to allowing slavery in Missouri

JAMES MONROE (1758–1831)

U.S. president at the time Missouri entered the Union

WILLIAM PLUMER JR. (1789–1854)

U.S. representative from New Hampshire who wrote detailed letters about the debate over Missouri

JAMES TALLMADGE JR. (1778–1853)

U.S. representative from New York who first proposed limiting slavery in Missouri as a condition for becoming a state

WANT TO KNOW MORE?

At the Library

Adler, David A. *Enemies of Slavery*. New York: Holiday House, 2004.

Anderson, Dale. *The Causes of the Civil War*. Milwaukee: World Almanac Library, 2004.

Bennett, Michelle. *Missouri*. New York: Benchmark Books, 2001.

Heinrichs, Ann. *Maine*. Minneapolis: Compass Point Books, 2004.

On the Web

For more information on the *Missouri Compromise*, use FactHound to track down Web sites related to this book.

1. Go to *www.facthound.com*

2. Type in a search word related to this book or this book ID: 075651634X

3. Click on the *Fetch It* button.

Your trusty FactHound will fetch the best Web sites for you!

On the Road

The U.S. Capitol
Washington, DC 20515
202/225-1908
Building where lawmakers debated
the Missouri Compromise

Missouri History Museum
Lindell and DeBaliviere in
Forest Park
St. Louis, MO 63112
314/746-4599
Exhibits on early Missouri history
and the lives of Missourians

Look for more We the People books about this era:

The Assassination of Abraham Lincoln
ISBN 0-7565-0678-6

The Battle of Gettysburg
ISBN 0-7565-0098-2

Battle of the Ironclads
ISBN 0-7565-1628-5

The Carpetbaggers
ISBN 0-7565-0834-7

The Emancipation Proclamation
ISBN 0-7565-0209-8

Fort Sumter
ISBN 0-7565-1629-3

The Gettysburg Address
ISBN 0-7565-1271-9

Great Women of the Civil War
ISBN 0-7565-0839-8

The Lincoln–Douglas Debates
ISBN 0-7565-1632-3

The Reconstruction Amendments
ISBN 0-7565-1636-6

Surrender at Appomattox
ISBN 0-7565-1626-9

The Underground Railroad
ISBN 0-7565-0102-4

A complete list of We the People titles is available on our Web site:
www.compasspointbooks.com

INDEX

About the Author

Michael Burgan is a freelance writer for children and adults. A history graduate of the University of Connecticut, he has written more than 90 fiction and nonfiction children's books for various publishers. For adult audiences, he has written news articles, essays, and plays. Michael Burgan is a recipient of an Educational Press Association of America award.